Updated Austria Travel Guide

Ruby Shawn

Updated Austria Travel Guide

A Comprehensive Guide to Explore the Rich History, iconic tourist spots, Natural Wonders, Vibrant Culture, and Stunning Landscapes of Austria and Travel Tips from Locals

By

Ruby Shawn

Disclaimer:

The information contained in this book is for general information purposes only. While we endeavor to keep the information up to date and correct, we make no representations or warranties of any kind, express or implied, about the completeness, accuracy, reliability, suitability, or availability with respect to the book or the information, products, services, or related graphics contained in the book for any purpose. Any reliance you place on such information is therefore strictly at your own risk.

In no event will we be liable for any loss or damage including without limitation, indirect or consequential loss or damage, or any loss or damage whatsoever arising from loss of data or profits arising out of, or in connection with, the use of this book.

Every effort has been made to ensure that the book complies with Austrian laws and regulations. However, the reader should always verify the information independently before acting on it.

Table of Content

Introduction

Austria is a small but beautiful country located in the heart of Europe, known for its stunning alpine landscapes, rich history, and vibrant culture. From the majestic peaks of the Austrian Alps to the grand architecture of Vienna, Austria has something to offer every traveler. Whether you are an adventure seeker looking for the perfect ski slopes, a history buff interested in the country's imperial past, or a foodie searching for the best schnitzel and strudel, Austria has it all.

This travel guide is designed to help you plan your trip to Austria and make the most of your time in this wonderful country. In the following pages, we will take you on a journey through Austria's most famous cities and regions, and introduce you to the many activities and experiences that await you here.

First, we will explore the vibrant capital city of Vienna, with its grand imperial palaces, world-class museums, and vibrant café culture. From here, we will take you to the picturesque city of Salzburg, the birthplace of Mozart and home to some of the country's most beautiful Baroque architecture. We will then head to the western region of Tyrol, with its dramatic mountain landscapes and charming alpine villages, perfect for outdoor activities such as skiing, hiking, and mountain biking.

Moving further east, we will explore the lakeside town of Hallstatt, with its stunning scenery and rich history dating back to the Iron Age. From here, we will take you to the spa town of Bad Ischl, a favorite holiday destination of Austria's imperial rulers, and home to some of the country's finest traditional cuisine.

Finally, we will venture into the eastern region of Styria, known for its rolling hills, vineyards, and thermal spas, and home to some of Austria's most delicious wines and culinary specialties.

Throughout the book, we will provide practical tips and advice on everything from transportation and accommodation to local customs and etiquette. We will also highlight some of Austria's lesser-known gems and off-the-beaten-path destinations, to help you discover the country's hidden treasures and experience its authentic local culture.

Whether you are a first-time visitor to Austria or a seasoned traveler, this guidebook will help you create the trip of a lifetime, filled with unforgettable experiences and memories that will last a lifetime. So sit back, relax, and let us take you on a journey through one of Europe's most enchanting destinations.

Geography

Austria, located in the heart of Europe, is a landlocked country bordered by Germany to the northwest, the Czech Republic to the north, Slovakia to the northeast, Hungary to the east, Slovenia and Italy to the south, and Switzerland and Liechtenstein to the west. With an area of 83,879 square kilometers, it is the 12th smallest country in Europe.

The country is predominantly mountainous, with the Alps covering about 62% of the country's total area. The highest peak in Austria is Grossglockner, which stands at 3,798 meters. The Danube is the country's largest river, and it flows eastward through the heart of Austria. Other significant rivers include the Mur, Inn, and Traun. Austria has over 200 lakes, with Lake Neusiedl being the largest. It is shared with Hungary and is a UNESCO World Heritage Site.

Austria's diverse landscape has given rise to a variety of ecosystems, including alpine and subalpine meadows, coniferous forests, and steppe grasslands. The country has a rich biodiversity, with over 47,000 recorded species of flora and fauna. The Hohe Tauern National Park, Austria's largest national park, is home to several rare and endangered species, including the golden eagle, the ibex, and the lynx.

Austria's climate is influenced by its position in the middle of Europe and its mountainous terrain. The country experiences a temperate continental climate with cold, snowy winters and warm summers. In the lower regions, the temperature can reach 30 degrees Celsius in summer, while in the mountains, it can drop below freezing point even in the summer months.

Austria has a rich geological history, with evidence of volcanic activity dating back to the Mesozoic Era. The country is also home to several mineral deposits, including iron ore, lignite, and magnesite. The salt mines in Hallstatt, which date back to the Bronze Age, are a UNESCO World Heritage Site.

Overall, Austria's unique geography has contributed to its cultural and historical significance. Its mountains, lakes, and forests have provided a stunning backdrop for its art, architecture, and music. Its climate has shaped its agriculture and outdoor recreation, while its geological history has played a vital role in its economic development.

History

The history of Austria is rich and diverse, with influences from the Celts, Romans, Germanic tribes, and the Habsburg monarchy. The country's strategic location at the crossroads of Europe has made it an important player in the continent's history.

The first evidence of human habitation in Austria dates back to the Paleolithic era, with artifacts found in the Danube Valley. The Celts arrived in the area around 400 BC and established settlements, followed by the Romans in the 1st century BC. The Roman Empire brought significant development and infrastructure to the region, including the construction of roads and aqueducts.

In the 6th century AD, the Germanic tribes, namely the Bavarians and the Avars, migrated to Austria and established their kingdoms. During the Middle Ages, Austria was part of the Holy Roman Empire, and the Babenberg dynasty ruled the region for several centuries. In the late 13th century, the Habsburg dynasty took control of Austria, and under their rule, the country became a major power in Europe.

During the Renaissance and Baroque periods, Austria flourished culturally and economically. The Habsburgs commissioned magnificent architecture, such as the Hofburg Palace in Vienna and Schönbrunn Palace, and were great patrons of the arts. Austria also played a significant role in the Counter-Reformation, which aimed to restore Catholicism in Europe.

In the 19th century, Austria became part of the Austro-Hungarian Empire, which was dissolved after World War I. Austria then became a republic, but its political stability was short-lived due to the rise of Nazism in neighboring Germany. Austria was annexed by Germany in 1938 and became a battleground during World War II. The country was liberated by Allied forces in 1945 and regained its independence.

Since then, Austria has rebuilt and developed into a prosperous and democratic country. It has played a role in the formation of the European Union and continues to be an important player in European politics and culture.

Today, Austria is known for its rich history, cultural heritage, and scenic beauty. Visitors to the country can experience its fascinating history through its museums, galleries, and architectural landmarks. The country's unique blend of traditional and modern culture is evident in its music, art, and culinary scene. Austria's stunning natural landscapes, including the Alps, lakes, and forests, attract millions of tourists every year.

Culture and people

Austria is a country with a rich culture and diverse population, shaped by its geography, history, and interactions with neighboring countries. The culture of Austria is strongly influenced by the country's location in central Europe, and its history as a multicultural empire that once encompassed much of central and eastern Europe. The people of Austria are known for their love of music, art, and cuisine, as well as their strong sense of national pride.

The culture of Austria is rooted in a rich tradition of music, art, and literature. Austria has produced some of the world's greatest composers, including Mozart, Beethoven, and Strauss, as well as many other notable figures in the arts. The country is also known for its architecture, which is characterized by the influence of the Baroque and Rococo styles. The Vienna Secession, a movement of artists and designers that emerged in the late 19th century, is also an important part of Austria's cultural heritage.

Austria has a diverse population, with people from many different ethnic and cultural backgrounds. The largest ethnic group is the Austrians, who make up around 90% of the population. Other significant ethnic groups include Germans, Turks, and Slovenes. Austria is also home to many immigrants from other parts of the world, including Eastern Europe, the Middle East, and Africa.

The people of Austria are known for their love of food and drink. Austrian cuisine is characterized by hearty, traditional dishes such as Wiener Schnitzel, Tafelspitz, and Apfelstrudel. The country is also famous for its coffeehouse culture, which dates back to the 17th century. Viennese coffeehouses are known for their relaxed atmosphere and their role as gathering places for intellectuals and artists.

Austria has a strong sense of national pride, which is reflected in its national symbols and traditions. The Austrian flag, which features red and white stripes and a coat of arms, is one of the oldest national flags in the world. Other national symbols include the coat of arms of the Austrian Republic, which features a double-headed eagle, and the national anthem, "Land of the Mountains, Land by the River."

Religion is an important part of Austrian culture, with around 73% of the population identifying as Roman Catholic. Other significant religions include Protestantism, Islam, and Judaism. The Catholic Church has played an important role in Austria's history and continues to be a significant cultural institution.

In addition to its rich cultural heritage, Austria is also known for its stunning natural beauty. The country is home to the Alps, one of the most iconic mountain ranges in the world, as well as many other breathtaking landscapes. The Danube River, which flows through Austria, is also a major natural attraction. Austria's natural beauty is an important part of the country's identity and is reflected in its tourism industry.

Overall, the culture and people of Austria are a fascinating and complex subject, shaped by a long and rich history, diverse population, and stunning natural beauty. Understanding the culture and people of Austria is an essential part of experiencing all that this incredible country has to offer. Whether you are interested in music, art, cuisine, or nature, Austria has something for everyone.

PLANNING YOUR TRIP TO

AUSTRIA

Planning a trip to Austria is an exciting prospect, as the country offers a wealth of cultural, historical, and natural attractions that are sure to captivate any visitor. From the imperial grandeur of Vienna to the Alpine splendor of Salzburg, Austria is a land of contrasts and diversity, with something to suit every taste and interest.

Before embarking on a trip to Austria, it is important to plan carefully to ensure that your visit is as enjoyable and stress-free as possible. This includes making decisions about transportation, accommodation, and sightseeing, as well as considering practical factors such as weather, currency exchange rates, and visa requirements.

This guide aims to provide a comprehensive overview of the key factors to consider when planning a trip to Austria. Whether you are a first-time visitor or a seasoned traveler, this guide will offer valuable insights and advice to help you make the most of your time in this beautiful and fascinating country.

Best time to visit

Austria is a country of rich culture and history, stunning landscapes, and charming cities that offer a plethora of activities and experiences to visitors. It is a year-round destination, with each season offering its unique attractions and charm. However, the best time to visit Austria depends on your preferences and interests.

Summer, from June to August, is the peak tourist season in Austria, and it is the best time to explore the country's alpine regions and lakes. The weather is generally warm and pleasant, making it ideal for outdoor activities such as hiking, cycling, swimming, and exploring the beautiful cities and villages. The days are long, with up to 16 hours of daylight, giving visitors more time to explore and enjoy the country's attractions. However, this is also the busiest time, and the popular destinations can get crowded and expensive.

Spring and fall are considered the shoulder seasons, and they offer visitors a quieter and more affordable travel experience. From mid-March to May and September to October, the weather is mild, and the crowds are thinner, making it an ideal time to explore the country's cultural attractions and enjoy outdoor activities such as hiking and cycling. The autumn season is particularly beautiful, with the changing colors of the foliage and the grape harvest festivals in the wine-growing regions.

Winter, from December to February, is the best time to visit Austria if you are a winter sports enthusiast. The country is home to some of the best skiing destinations in the world, and the snow-covered landscapes are simply magical. The Christmas markets in Vienna and Salzburg are also a must-visit during the festive season, and the cities' streets are beautifully decorated with lights and ornaments.

It is essential to keep in mind that Austria's weather can be unpredictable, and it is advisable to pack for all seasons, regardless of when you plan to visit. Also, the peak tourist season means higher prices and more crowds, so if you prefer a more relaxed and budget-friendly trip, it is best to visit during the shoulder seasons.

The best time to visit Austria depends on your interests and preferences. Whether you want to explore the alpine regions, enjoy outdoor activities, experience the country's culture and history, or indulge in winter sports, Austria has something to offer year-round. Plan your trip accordingly, keeping in mind the weather, crowds, and prices, and you are guaranteed to have a memorable and enjoyable trip to Austria.

Visa requirements

When planning a trip to Austria, it's essential to understand the visa requirements that apply to your situation. Austria is a member of the Schengen Area, which means that visitors from certain countries can enter Austria without a visa for up to 90 days within a six-month period. The visa-free entry applies to citizens of the European Union (EU) and the European Economic Area (EEA), as well as Switzerland, Canada, the United States, Australia, and New Zealand.

If you are not a citizen of any of the visa-free countries, you will need to apply for a Schengen visa at an Austrian embassy or consulate in your home country. The visa application process usually takes several weeks, so it's essential to plan accordingly. You will need to provide various documents, including a valid passport, proof of travel insurance, and proof of accommodation in Austria.

It's worth noting that some travelers may be eligible for an eVisa, which can be applied for online. However, not all countries are eligible for this option, so it's important to check before making any travel arrangements.

For those who plan to work or study in Austria, a different type of visa is required. You will need to apply for a national visa, which allows you to stay in Austria for a more extended period. The application process for a national visa is more complicated and time-consuming than the Schengen visa, and you may need to provide additional documents, such as proof of enrollment in a university or evidence of a job offer.

It's important to note that visa requirements can change at any time, so it's always a good idea to check with the Austrian embassy or consulate in your home country before making any travel arrangements.

In addition to the visa requirements, it's also essential to have a valid passport that will not expire within six months of your planned departure from Austria. If your passport is due to expire before then, you will need to renew it before applying for a visa.

Overall, while navigating the visa requirements can be daunting, the process is relatively straightforward and can be managed with proper planning and preparation. With the necessary documents in hand, you can focus on enjoying your trip to Austria without worrying about any visa-related issues.

Currency and exchange rates

Currency and exchange rates are essential to consider when planning a trip to Austria. Austria is a member of the European Union and the Eurozone, which means that the official currency is the euro. The euro is used by 19 of the 27 member states of the European Union, making it the second most widely used currency in the world after the US dollar. The euro is subdivided into 100 cents.

When it comes to exchanging currency, it is recommended to do so in Austria rather than in your home country. Banks and exchange offices offer competitive exchange rates, but keep in mind that exchange rates at airports and tourist areas are typically less favorable. ATMs are widely available throughout Austria and offer a convenient way to withdraw euros with your debit card. However, check with your bank regarding any foreign transaction fees or ATM fees that may apply.

Credit and debit cards are widely accepted in Austria, especially in larger cities and tourist areas. Visa and Mastercard are the most commonly accepted credit cards, while American Express and Discover may be less widely accepted. Be sure to inform your bank of your travel plans to avoid any issues with card transactions while in Austria.

Austria is generally a safe country for travelers, and incidents of theft and scams are relatively low. However, it is still important to be aware of common scams and take precautions to protect your personal belongings. Keep your passport and valuables in a secure location, and be cautious of pickpockets in crowded areas such as public transportation and tourist sites.

When it comes to tipping, it is customary to leave a small tip for good service in Austria. In restaurants, a tip of 5-10% is common, while rounding up to the nearest euro is common for smaller transactions. Tipping is not necessary for services such as taxis or hairdressers, but rounding up to the nearest euro is appreciated.

Overall, understanding the currency and exchange rates in Austria is crucial for a smooth and enjoyable trip. Be sure to plan ahead and budget accordingly to make the most of your time in this beautiful country.

Health and safety

When traveling to Austria, it's important to consider your health and safety to ensure a stress-free and enjoyable trip. Here are some tips to keep in mind:

Medical Insurance: If you are a foreigner traveling to Austria, it is highly recommended to purchase travel insurance that includes medical coverage. Austria has excellent medical facilities, but medical treatment can be expensive for those without insurance.

Emergency Services: Austria has a well-developed emergency response system, and the emergency number for police, fire, and ambulance is 112.

Tap Water: Austria has excellent tap water, and it is safe to drink in most parts of the country. However, it is always best to check with locals or your accommodation provider.

Sun Protection: Austria has a temperate climate, but during the summer months, temperatures can rise, and the sun can be strong. Remember to wear sunscreen, a hat, and sunglasses to protect yourself from the sun.

Safety in the Mountains: Austria is known for its stunning mountain ranges, and many travelers come to the country to hike and ski. However, it is important to exercise caution and be aware of your surroundings, especially in the more remote areas. Always follow the designated hiking trails, bring a map, and dress appropriately for the weather.

Crime: Austria is generally a safe country to visit, with a low crime rate. However, as with any destination, it's important to take precautions and be aware of your surroundings, especially in crowded areas and tourist hotspots.

Food Safety: Austria has a rich culinary culture, and travelers should try the local cuisine. However, it's important to exercise caution when it comes to food safety. Be careful of consuming raw or undercooked meat, seafood, and eggs, and always wash your hands before eating.

Road Safety: If you plan on driving in Austria, be aware that the roads can be narrow and winding in some areas. Always wear your seatbelt, adhere to speed limits, and don't drink and drive.

By following these simple tips, you can ensure a safe and healthy trip to Austria. Remember to also check the latest travel advisories before your trip to stay up-to-date on any potential health or safety risks.

Language and communication

Austria is a country with a rich cultural heritage and history, and it is a popular tourist destination for people from all over the world. When traveling to Austria, it is essential to have some knowledge of the local language and communication etiquette to make the most of your trip. In this article, we will explore the language and communication in Austria.

The official language of Austria is German, and it is the primary language spoken by the majority of the population. However, Austria also has several other regional languages, such as Slovenian, Croatian, and Hungarian, which are spoken in different parts of the country. English is also widely spoken, particularly in major tourist destinations, and many people in Austria are fluent in multiple languages.

When traveling to Austria, it is a good idea to learn some basic German phrases to help you communicate with locals. Simple greetings such as "Guten Morgen" (good morning), "Guten Tag" (good afternoon), and "Guten Abend" (good evening) can go a long way in building a rapport with locals. It is also useful to learn some common phrases such as "Entschuldigung" (excuse me), "Danke" (thank you), and "Bitte" (please).

In Austria, the communication style is relatively formal, particularly when interacting with people in professional settings. It is important to address people using their titles, such as "Herr" (Mr.), "Frau" (Mrs.), or "Fräulein" (Miss), followed by their surname. This formality is also reflected in written communication, such as emails or letters, where it is customary to use formal language and avoid using colloquialisms or slang.

Austrians value punctuality, and it is essential to arrive on time for appointments and meetings. It is also considered polite to confirm appointments or reservations a few days in advance, particularly for formal occasions. When making plans with Austrians, it is crucial to be clear and specific about the time, place, and other details to avoid confusion.

Austrians are generally reserved and polite in their communication style, and it is essential to be respectful of their personal space and boundaries. It is considered impolite to invade someone's personal space, such as standing too close or touching them, without permission. When interacting with strangers or people in public places, it is customary to keep a respectful distance and avoid making prolonged eye contact.

When it comes to nonverbal communication, Austrians are relatively reserved and do not use many hand gestures or facial expressions in their communication. However, they place great importance on body language and posture, and it is essential to maintain a professional and respectful demeanor, particularly in formal settings.

In terms of communication technology, Austria has a well-developed telecommunications infrastructure, and most hotels and public spaces offer free Wi-Fi access. It is also easy to purchase a local SIM card for your phone or tablet, which will give you access to local data and voice services. Austria has excellent mobile coverage, particularly in urban areas, and most mobile providers offer prepaid and postpaid plans that cater to different usage patterns and budgets.

When traveling to Austria, it is essential to have some knowledge of the local language and communication etiquette to help you make the most of your trip. Learning some basic German phrases and being respectful of local customs and communication styles can go a long way in building rapport and creating memorable experiences. Austria is a beautiful and culturally rich country, and by being respectful and attentive to local customs and communication styles, you can have a truly unforgettable experience.

GETTING AROUND

AUSTRIA

Getting around Austria is relatively easy and convenient, thanks to the country's efficient and reliable transportation system. Whether you're exploring the cities or heading out to the countryside, there are plenty of options to choose from, including trains, buses, trams, and taxis. In this section, we'll take a closer look at the various modes of transportation available in Austria and offer tips on how to navigate the country like a local.

Public Transportation

Austria has an extensive public transportation network that covers the entire country. The system is well-developed and efficient, making it easy to get around even if you don't speak the language. The most common mode of public transport in Austria is the train, which connects major cities and smaller towns alike. The Austrian Federal Railways (ÖBB) operate the trains and offer a variety of services, including regional, intercity, and high-speed trains. The trains are clean, comfortable, and usually on time, and the fares are relatively affordable. You can purchase tickets at the train station, online, or through the ÖBB app.

In addition to trains, Austria also has an extensive network of buses and trams, which are operated by various companies depending on the region. Buses are generally cheaper than trains and cover a wider area, making them ideal for exploring smaller towns and villages. Trams, on the other hand, are more common in urban areas, such as Vienna, Graz, and Linz. They are an efficient and convenient way to get around the city, with frequent services and a reliable schedule.

Taxis

Taxis are widely available in Austria, and they are a convenient option if you want to get around quickly or if you're traveling with a group. Taxis are metered, and the fares are regulated by the government, so you can expect a fair price. However, taxis are generally more expensive than public transport, and you may have to wait in line at busy times.

Bike Rental

Austria is a great place for cycling, with miles of dedicated bike paths and scenic routes through the countryside. Renting a bike is an excellent way to explore the local area at your own pace, and it's also a great way to get some exercise. Many cities, including Vienna, offer bike rental schemes, which are easy to use and affordable. You can also rent bikes from local bike shops and hotels, and there are plenty of guided tours available if you prefer to explore with a group.

Driving

If you want to explore the more remote parts of Austria, driving is a good option. The country has a well-maintained road network, with well-signposted routes and clear road markings. However, driving in Austria can be challenging, especially in urban areas, where traffic can be heavy and parking is limited. You'll also need to be aware of the local driving laws, such as speed limits and road signs, which may be different from those in your home country. If you plan to rent a car, make sure you have a valid driving license and that you're familiar with the local driving regulations.

Getting around Austria is relatively easy and convenient, thanks to the country's well-developed transportation system. Whether you prefer public transport or driving, there are plenty of options available to suit your needs and budget. With a little planning and preparation, you can explore all that Austria has to offer and create memories that will last a lifetime.

Walking And Hiking In Austria

Austria is a country famous for its majestic mountains and stunning landscapes, making it an ideal destination for walking and hiking enthusiasts. From gentle strolls in the rolling hills to challenging ascents up snow-capped peaks, Austria has something for everyone.

One of the most popular hiking areas in Austria is the Austrian Alps, which stretches across the country. The Alps offer some of the most beautiful and dramatic scenery in Europe, with towering peaks, crystal-clear lakes, and dense forests. There are many hiking trails to choose from, ranging from easy walks to challenging multi-day treks.

The Austrian Alps are home to many of Austria's highest mountains, including the Grossglockner, the highest mountain in Austria, and the Zugspitze, which is the highest peak in Germany. The Grossglockner is part of the Hohe Tauern National Park, which is the largest nature reserve in the Alps. The park is a paradise for walkers and hikers, with over 350 kilometers of marked trails to explore.

Another popular hiking area in Austria is the Salzkammergut region, which is famous for its stunning lakes and mountains. The Salzkammergut is a region of outstanding natural beauty, with crystal-clear lakes, rolling hills, and snow-capped peaks. The region is also famous for its traditional Austrian architecture, which is characterized by wooden chalets and colorful flower boxes.

The Salzkammergut is home to many hiking trails, including the 340-kilometer long Salzkammergut Trail, which takes hikers through some of the most beautiful parts of the region. The trail passes through charming villages, pastures, and forests, and offers stunning views of the surrounding mountains.

In addition to the Austrian Alps and the Salzkammergut, there are many other areas of Austria that are perfect for walking and hiking. The Wachau Valley, which is a UNESCO World Heritage Site, is a beautiful area of vineyards and fruit orchards, and offers many walking trails that take hikers through picturesque villages and along the banks of the Danube River.

The Tyrol region is another popular hiking area, with many trails that lead through stunning alpine landscapes. The Tyrol is also home to some of the most famous hiking routes in the world, including the Eagle's Walk, which is a long-distance trail that covers 412 kilometers and takes hikers through some of the most beautiful parts of the region.

No matter where you choose to hike in Austria, there are a few things to keep in mind to ensure a safe and enjoyable trip. First, be sure to wear appropriate clothing and footwear, as the weather can change quickly in the mountains. It's also a good idea to bring a map and compass or GPS, as well as plenty of food and water.

It's important to respect the natural environment while hiking in Austria. Stay on marked trails, avoid damaging plants and wildlife, and do not litter. Finally, be aware of your limitations and do not attempt hikes that are beyond your fitness level.

Overall, walking and hiking in Austria is a great way to explore the country's stunning landscapes and enjoy the great outdoors. With so many trails to choose from, there is something for hikers of all abilities, from gentle walks to challenging mountain treks. Just be sure to plan ahead, pack appropriately, and respect the natural environment, and you're sure to have a memorable hiking experience in Austria.

ACCOMMODATION

OPTIONS IN AUSTRIA

Austria is a popular tourist destination for its stunning natural beauty, rich history, and cultural heritage. As such, it offers a wide range of accommodation options to suit different budgets, preferences, and travel styles. Whether you're looking for luxury hotels, quaint guesthouses, cozy bed and breakfasts, or affordable hostels, Austria has something for everyone.

One of the great things about traveling in Austria is that the country is relatively small and easy to get around, so you can explore different regions and cities while staying in a variety of accommodations. From the charming streets of Vienna to the majestic peaks of the Alps, Austria has a diverse range of destinations and experiences to offer. In this section, we'll explore some of the most popular types of accommodation in Austria, as well as some tips on how to find the right one for your trip.

Hotels And Resorts

Austria offers a diverse range of accommodation options for visitors, from luxurious hotels and resorts to affordable guesthouses and hostels. When it comes to hotels and resorts, Austria boasts some of the best in Europe, with many properties offering breathtaking views of the Alps, spa facilities, and gourmet dining options. With so many options to choose from, it can be overwhelming to decide on the perfect place to stay during your trip. Here are some tips on using hotels and resorts while in Austria and how to locate the good ones.

One of the best ways to find good hotels and resorts in Austria is to do some research online. Travel websites such as TripAdvisor, Booking.com, and Expedia offer a wealth of information on hotels and resorts in Austria, including user reviews, ratings, and photos. These websites allow you to filter your search by price range, location, and amenities, making it easy to find the perfect property to suit your needs.

It is also important to consider the location of the hotel or resort. If you plan to explore the cities and towns of Austria, you may want to look for properties that are centrally located, with easy access to public transportation. If you are interested in outdoor activities such as skiing or hiking, you may want to look for properties that are located near the mountains.

When it comes to choosing a hotel or resort, it is important to read reviews from other travelers to get a sense of the quality of the property. Look for reviews that mention cleanliness, customer service, and the overall experience of staying at the property. It is also a good idea to check the hotel's website to see what amenities and services are offered. Some hotels and resorts may offer complimentary breakfast, spa facilities, or on-site dining options, which can add value to your stay.

Another factor to consider when choosing a hotel or resort in Austria is the price. While some properties can be quite expensive, there are also many affordable options available, particularly in smaller towns and cities. Keep in mind that prices may fluctuate depending on the time of year and the popularity of the property, so it is a good idea to book in advance if you are traveling during peak season.

If you are looking for a more luxurious experience, Austria offers many high-end hotels and resorts that cater to discerning travelers. These properties often offer exceptional amenities such as indoor and outdoor pools, gourmet restaurants, and exclusive spa facilities. However, these properties can also be quite expensive, with prices ranging from several hundred to several thousand euros per night.

In addition to hotels and resorts, Austria also offers a range of alternative accommodation options, such as vacation rentals, bed and breakfasts, and hostels. Vacation rentals can be a great option for families or groups traveling together, as they offer more space and privacy than a hotel room. Bed and breakfasts are also a popular choice, particularly in smaller towns and villages, and offer a more intimate and personalized experience. Hostels are a good choice for budget-conscious travelers, offering affordable dormitory-style accommodation with shared facilities.

Austria offers a wide variety of accommodation options for visitors, from luxurious hotels and resorts to affordable guesthouses and hostels. When choosing a hotel or resort, it is important to do your research, read reviews, and consider factors such as location, amenities, and price. By following these tips, you can find the perfect place to stay during your trip to Austria.

Vacation rentals

Vacation rentals, such as apartments and houses, are becoming increasingly popular for travelers in Austria. They offer more space, privacy, and often more affordable options than traditional hotels. Here's how to find a good vacation rental in Austria.

Firstly, it's important to decide on the location of your vacation rental. Austria has many beautiful regions, from the Alps to Vienna, each with their own unique culture and attractions. Do some research on the areas you want to visit and look for vacation rentals in those areas.

There are several websites that list vacation rentals in Austria, such as Airbnb, Booking.com, and VRBO. These websites allow you to search for properties by location, price, and amenities. They also have reviews from previous guests, which can be a good indicator of the quality of the property.

When choosing a vacation rental, consider the amenities offered. Does the rental have a kitchen? A washer and dryer? A pool or hot tub? These amenities can make your stay more comfortable and convenient.

It's also important to consider the size of the rental. Make sure it's large enough to accommodate your group comfortably. Some vacation rentals may have restrictions on the number of guests allowed, so be sure to check the listing carefully.

When booking a vacation rental, it's important to read the terms and conditions carefully. Make sure you understand the cancellation policy, payment schedule, and any other fees that may be charged. Some vacation rentals may require a security deposit, which will be refunded after your stay if there is no damage to the property.

If you have any questions or concerns about the vacation rental, don't hesitate to contact the owner or property manager. They can provide more information and help you make an informed decision.

One thing to keep in mind when using vacation rentals in Austria is that they may not have the same level of service as a traditional hotel. You won't have daily housekeeping, for example, and there may not be a front desk staff available 24/7. However, many vacation rentals do offer keyless entry and self check-in, which can be convenient for travelers.

Overall, using vacation rentals in Austria can be a great way to experience the country like a local. With a little research and careful planning, you can find a comfortable and affordable vacation rental that meets your needs.

Camping and RVs

Camping and RVing in Austria is a popular way to experience the country's natural beauty and outdoor activities. From the stunning alpine scenery to the picturesque lakes and rivers, there is no shortage of camping and RV sites to choose from. In this guide, we will explore the different options available for camping and RVing in Austria and provide tips on how to locate the best ones.

Camping is a popular option for those who want to experience the great outdoors in Austria. There are a variety of camping sites located throughout the country, ranging from basic tent camping to more luxurious options with amenities such as electricity and hot showers. Many of these campsites are located in or near Austria's national parks and other natural attractions, offering easy access to hiking, biking, and other outdoor activities.

One popular camping option in Austria is the "Alm camping," where campers stay on high mountain pastures during the summer months. These campsites are often only accessible by hiking or using a 4x4 vehicle, adding to the sense of adventure and seclusion. The campsites are basic, with no electricity or running water, but the stunning views and fresh mountain air make it all worth it.

For those who prefer a bit more comfort, there are also RV parks and campgrounds with more amenities. Many of these sites offer electrical and water hookups, as well as laundry facilities and shower blocks. Some even have swimming pools, restaurants, and other on-site activities.

When it comes to locating the best camping and RV sites in Austria, there are a few things to consider. Firstly, it's important to research the location and surroundings of the site to ensure it fits your needs and interests. For example, if you're looking for a peaceful, secluded getaway, a remote mountain camping spot might be ideal. On the other hand, if you want to be close to urban areas and cultural attractions, a campground near a major city might be a better fit.

It's also important to check the facilities and amenities available at the site. Some campsites may only offer basic facilities, while others have a range of amenities like swimming pools, restaurants, and shops. You should also check the site's policies on pets, noise, and other rules to ensure it aligns with your needs and preferences.

Finally, it's a good idea to read reviews from previous campers to get an idea of what to expect. Online review sites like TripAdvisor and Yelp can be a useful tool for finding the best camping and RV sites in Austria, as they allow you to read firsthand accounts of other campers' experiences.

Overall, camping and RVing in Austria is a great way to experience the country's natural beauty and outdoor activities. Whether you prefer tent camping in remote mountain locations or RVing in more luxurious campgrounds, there are plenty of options available to suit every budget and interest. By doing your research and reading reviews from other travelers, you can find the perfect camping or RV site for your next trip to Austria.

EXPLORING AUSTRIA

Austria is a country that boasts a rich cultural heritage, breathtaking natural scenery, and a fascinating history. The country is located in the heart of Europe, bordered by Germany, the Czech Republic, Slovakia, Hungary, Slovenia, Italy, Switzerland, and Liechtenstein. From the stunning mountain ranges of the Austrian Alps to the picturesque villages and cities dotted throughout the country, there is something for everyone in Austria.

Whether you are interested in exploring the rich cultural heritage of Austria's cities, hiking in the mountains, or simply relaxing in one of the country's many spa towns, Austria has something to offer. With its friendly people, excellent cuisine, and wide range of activities, Austria is the perfect destination for anyone looking to explore all that Europe has to offer. In this section, we will explore some of the best ways to explore Austria and make the most of your time in this beautiful country.

Top Destinations in Austria

Austria is a beautiful country in the heart of Europe with a rich history and a diverse landscape. From stunning alpine peaks to picturesque villages, Austria is a destination that has something to offer for everyone. Here are the top destinations in Austria that you should not miss:

Vienna - The Capital City

Vienna is the capital and largest city in Austria, known for its rich history, stunning architecture, and vibrant cultural scene. The city is home to many museums, art galleries, and theaters, making it an ideal destination for culture lovers. Don't miss a visit to the Schönbrunn Palace, the Hofburg Palace, and the Vienna State Opera House.

Salzburg - Birthplace of Mozart

Salzburg is a charming city located in the north of Austria and is best known as the birthplace of Wolfgang Amadeus Mozart. The city is home to many stunning baroque buildings, such as the Salzburg Cathedral and the Mirabell Palace. The Hohensalzburg Fortress, perched on a hill above the city, is also worth a visit.

Innsbruck - The Capital of the Alps

Innsbruck is a beautiful city located in the western part of Austria, known for its stunning alpine scenery and vibrant cultural scene. The city is home to many museums, galleries, and theaters, making it an ideal destination for culture lovers. Don't miss a visit to the Hofkirche, the Imperial Palace, and the Swarovski Crystal Worlds.

Hallstatt - A Fairytale Village

Hallstatt is a charming village located in the heart of the Austrian Alps, known for its stunning scenery and picturesque architecture. The village is situated on the shores of Lake Hallstatt and is surrounded by towering mountains, making it an ideal destination for nature lovers. Don't miss a visit to the Hallstatt Salt Mine, one of the oldest salt mines in the world.

Zell am See - A Scenic Lakeside Town

Zell am See is a picturesque town located in the Salzburg region of Austria, known for its stunning alpine scenery and scenic lakeside location. The town is home to many outdoor activities, including hiking, skiing, and water sports. Don't miss a visit to the Zell am See-Kaprun ski resort, one of the best ski resorts in Austria.

Graz - A Cultural Capital

Graz is a beautiful city located in the south of Austria, known for its stunning architecture, vibrant cultural scene, and rich history.

The city is home to many museums, galleries, and theaters, making it an ideal destination for culture lovers. Don't miss a visit to the Graz Clock Tower, the Graz Opera House, and the Schlossberg.

Kitzbühel - A Skiing Paradise

Kitzbühel is a charming town located in the Austrian Alps, known for its world-class skiing and stunning alpine scenery. The town is home to many ski resorts, making it an ideal destination for skiers and snowboarders. Don't miss a visit to the Kitzbüheler Horn, one of the most popular ski slopes in Austria.

Wachau Valley - A Scenic Wine Region

The Wachau Valley is a beautiful wine region located in the Danube Valley in Lower Austria, known for its stunning scenery, picturesque towns, and delicious wines. The region is home to many wineries and vineyards, making it an ideal destination for wine lovers. Don't miss a visit to the Melk Abbey, a stunning baroque monastery located on a hill overlooking the Danube River.

Historical And Cultural Sites

Austria is a country rich in history and culture, and there are numerous historical and cultural sites to visit. From ancient Roman ruins to imperial palaces and baroque churches, there is something for everyone. Here are some of the top historical and cultural sites in Austria:

1. Schönbrunn Palace

Located in Vienna, the Schönbrunn Palace was the summer residence of the Habsburg monarchs. This baroque palace and its gardens are a UNESCO World Heritage Site and one of the most popular tourist attractions in Austria.

2. Hofburg Palace

Another imperial palace in Vienna, the Hofburg Palace was the residence of the Habsburgs until the end of World War I. Today, it houses several museums, including the Sisi Museum and the Imperial Treasury.

3. Salzburg Old Town

The historic center of Salzburg is a UNESCO World Heritage Site and features numerous medieval and baroque buildings, including the Salzburg Cathedral and the Hohensalzburg Fortress.

4. Hallstatt

This picturesque town in the Austrian Alps is known for its salt mines, which have been in operation since the prehistoric era. The town's historic center is a UNESCO World Heritage Site and features traditional Austrian architecture.

5. Melk Abbey

Located in the Wachau Valley, the Melk Abbey is a baroque monastery that dates back to the 11th century. The abbey is renowned for its library, which contains more than 80,000 volumes.

6. St. Stephen's Cathedral

This Gothic cathedral is the symbol of Vienna and one of the most important religious buildings in Austria. It features stunning stained glass windows and a beautiful tower that offers panoramic views of the city.

7. Mozart's Birthplace

Located in Salzburg, the birthplace of Wolfgang Amadeus Mozart is now a museum dedicated to the composer's life and work. Visitors can see some of Mozart's original manuscripts and personal belongings.

8. Belvedere Palace

This baroque palace in Vienna was built in the early 18th century as the summer residence of Prince Eugene of Savoy. Today, it houses the Austrian Gallery, which features works by Austrian artists such as Gustav Klimt and Egon Schiele.

9. Innsbruck Old Town

The historic center of Innsbruck features numerous medieval and baroque buildings, including the Golden Roof, a famous landmark that was built in the 15th century.

10. Krems

This small town in the Wachau Valley is known for its wine and historic buildings, including the Gozzoburg Castle and the Steiner Tor, a medieval gate that is one of the last remaining structures of the town's former city walls.

These are just a few of the many historical and cultural sites in Austria. Whether you're interested in art, architecture, or history, Austria has something to offer.

Natural wonders

Austria is well-known for its stunning natural beauty, from towering mountains to sparkling lakes and pristine forests. The country is a paradise for nature lovers, and visitors are spoiled for choice when it comes to exploring its natural wonders. Here are some of the top natural wonders in Austria.

The Austrian Alps

The Austrian Alps are one of the most breathtaking natural wonders in the country, offering spectacular views, hiking trails, skiing and snowboarding opportunities, and more. The Alps cover around 62% of Austria, and visitors can explore a range of mountain ranges, including the Eastern Alps, the Central Alps, and the Southern Alps. Some of the most popular spots in the Austrian Alps include the Hohe Tauern National Park, the Kitzbühel Alps, and the Dachstein Mountains.

The Danube River

The Danube River is one of the most iconic waterways in Europe, and it flows through Austria, as well as nine other countries. The river is the second-longest in Europe, stretching over 1,770 miles, and it is a vital source of transportation, irrigation, and hydroelectric power. Visitors can take a river cruise along the Danube to explore its stunning landscapes, visit historic towns and cities along its banks, and experience the unique culture and cuisine of the region.

Lake Wolfgang

Located in the Salzkammergut region of Austria, Lake Wolfgang is a beautiful freshwater lake surrounded by scenic mountains and forests. The lake is a popular spot for swimming, fishing, boating, and hiking, and it is surrounded by charming towns and villages, such as St. Wolfgang and St. Gilgen. Visitors can take a boat ride across the lake, enjoy a picnic on the shore, or hike to the top of the Schafberg Mountain for stunning views.

Eisriesenwelt Ice Cave

The Eisriesenwelt Ice Cave is the largest ice cave in the world, stretching over 30 miles and featuring spectacular ice formations, such as stalactites and stalagmites. The cave is located in the Tennengebirge Mountains, and visitors can take a guided tour to explore its frozen wonders. The cave is open to visitors from May to October.

Krimml Waterfalls

The Krimml Waterfalls are the highest waterfalls in Austria, with a total drop of over 1,200 feet. The falls are located in the Hohe Tauern National Park, and visitors can take a hiking trail to explore the falls from different angles. The falls are also illuminated at night, creating a magical and romantic atmosphere.

Grossglockner High Alpine Road

The Grossglockner High Alpine Road is a scenic drive that winds through the Austrian Alps, offering stunning views of mountains, glaciers, and valleys. The road is around 30 miles long and includes 36 hairpin turns, making it a thrilling and exciting drive. Visitors can also stop at various viewpoints and rest areas along the road to take in the breathtaking scenery.

Zell am See

Zell am See is a charming town located on the shore of Lake Zell, surrounded by mountains and forests. The town is a popular destination for skiing and snowboarding in the winter, and hiking and water sports in the summer. Visitors can explore the town's historic center, visit the Zell am See-Kaprun ski resort, or take a boat ride on the lake.

Adventure Activities

Austria is a perfect destination for adventure lovers. It offers a diverse range of activities for all levels of adventure seekers. From the majestic Alps to the lush green forests, Austria has something for everyone. Here are some of the top adventure activities that one can experience while in Austria:

1. Skiing and Snowboarding

Austria is known for its incredible skiing and snowboarding slopes, and it's one of the most popular winter destinations in Europe. The Austrian Alps offer an extensive network of ski resorts, with some of the best ski slopes in the world. The slopes cater to all levels of skiers and snowboarders, from beginners to experts.

2. Hiking and Trekking

Austria has a vast network of hiking trails that cater to all levels of hikers. The trails pass through some of the most scenic landscapes in the world, from the majestic mountains to the picturesque valleys. Hiking in Austria is an excellent way to explore the country's natural beauty and enjoy the fresh mountain air.

3. Mountain Biking

Austria is a perfect destination for mountain bikers. The country has an extensive network of mountain biking trails that cater to all levels of riders. The trails offer incredible views of the mountains, forests, and lakes. Mountain biking in Austria is an excellent way to explore the countryside and stay fit.

4. Paragliding

Austria is a perfect destination for paragliding enthusiasts. The country has some of the most spectacular paragliding spots in the world, from the mountains to the lakes. Paragliding in Austria is an exhilarating experience, and the views are breathtaking.

5. Rafting and Kayaking

Austria is a perfect destination for water sports enthusiasts. The country has some of the most exciting rivers and lakes for rafting and kayaking. The rivers offer different levels of difficulty, from beginners to experts. Rafting and kayaking in Austria are an excellent way to enjoy the country's natural beauty and get an adrenaline rush.

6. Caving

Austria has a vast network of caves, and it's an excellent destination for caving enthusiasts. The caves offer a unique experience of exploring the underground world. The country has some of the most spectacular caves in the world, with stunning rock formations and underground rivers.

7. Climbing

Austria is a perfect destination for rock climbing enthusiasts. The country has some of the most spectacular rock climbing spots in the world, from the majestic mountains to the lush forests. Climbing in Austria is an excellent way to challenge yourself and enjoy the country's natural beauty.

8. Canyoning

Austria is a perfect destination for canyoning enthusiasts. The country has some of the most exciting canyoning spots in the world, from the gorges to the waterfalls. Canyoning in Austria is an exhilarating experience, and the views are breathtaking.

9. Zip-lining

Austria is a perfect destination for zip-lining enthusiasts. The country has some of the most spectacular zip-lining spots in the world, from the mountains to the forests. Zip-lining in Austria is an excellent way to enjoy the country's natural beauty and get an adrenaline rush.

10. Horseback Riding

Austria is a perfect destination for horseback riding enthusiasts. The country has some of the most picturesque riding trails in the world, from the mountains to the forests. Horseback riding in Austria is an excellent way to explore the countryside and enjoy the fresh air.

Dining and Drinking in Austria

Austria is a country renowned for its rich cultural heritage and stunning natural scenery, but it's also known for its exceptional cuisine and drink culture. From hearty traditional dishes to fine dining experiences, Austria has something for everyone when it comes to dining and drinking. In this article, we will explore some of the best culinary delights and drinking experiences you can enjoy in Austria.

Let's start with the country's national dish, Wiener Schnitzel. This breaded veal cutlet is a must-try when in Austria. The dish is traditionally served with a side of potato salad and lemon wedges. The key to a good Wiener Schnitzel is the meat, which should be pounded thin and tenderized before being coated in breadcrumbs and fried until golden brown. You can find this dish in almost every restaurant in Austria, but for an authentic experience, head to the city of Vienna, where the dish originated.

Another dish that you shouldn't miss when in Austria is Tafelspitz. This is a boiled beef dish that's typically served with horseradish sauce and apple-horseradish sauce, as well as boiled vegetables such as carrots, turnips, and potatoes. The beef is slow-cooked for several hours, resulting in a tender and flavorful meat that's perfect for a hearty meal.

If you're in the mood for something lighter, try the traditional Austrian soup, Frittatensuppe. This soup is made with a clear beef broth and thin pancake strips, which are rolled up and sliced before being added to the soup. The soup is often garnished with chives, and it's a popular choice for lunch or as a starter before a main course.

For dessert, Austria has many sweet treats to offer, but the most famous one is undoubtedly the Sachertorte. This chocolate cake was invented in Vienna in 1832, and it has become a symbol of Austrian cuisine. The cake is made with layers of dense chocolate cake, apricot jam, and chocolate ganache. It's typically served with a dollop of whipped cream and a cup of Viennese coffee.

Speaking of coffee, Austria is a country that takes its coffee culture very seriously. Vienna has a long tradition of coffeehouses, and the city is home to some of the most famous ones in the world. Café Central, for example, has been around since 1876 and was a favorite spot for intellectuals such as Sigmund Freud and Leon Trotsky. The coffeehouse serves a wide range of coffee blends, as well as pastries and light meals.

If you're more of a tea person, you should check out Demmer Teehaus. This teahouse has been around since 1888 and is a favorite among locals and tourists alike. They have an extensive selection of teas from all over the world, as well as sweet and savory snacks.

When it comes to drinking, Austria is famous for its wine. The country has a long history of winemaking, with the first vineyards dating back to Roman times. Austria's wine regions are scattered throughout the country, and they produce a variety of white and red wines. Some of the most famous wine regions include Wachau, Kamptal, and Burgenland.

If you're a beer lover, don't worry – Austria has plenty of options for you too. The country has a thriving beer culture, with many local breweries producing a wide range of beers. One of the most famous beers is Gösser, which has been around since 1860. The brewery offers tours where you can learn about the brewing process and sample some of their beers.

Austrian cuisine

Austria is a country with a rich culinary heritage, and its cuisine is a fusion of influences from neighboring countries such as Germany, Italy, and Hungary. Austrian cuisine is known for its hearty and flavorful dishes that are perfect for cold winter days or as comfort food.

One of the most famous dishes from Austria is Wiener Schnitzel. This breaded veal cutlet is a staple in Austrian cuisine and is enjoyed by locals and tourists alike. The dish is made with thinly sliced veal that is pounded flat and coated in breadcrumbs before being fried until golden brown. The dish is traditionally served with a side of potato salad and lemon wedges.

Another popular dish is Tafelspitz, a boiled beef dish that's typically served with horseradish sauce and apple-horseradish sauce, as well as boiled vegetables such as carrots, turnips, and potatoes. The beef is slow-cooked for several hours, resulting in a tender and flavorful meat that's perfect for a hearty meal.

For those who prefer lighter fare, there are plenty of soups to choose from. One of the most famous soups is Frittatensuppe, which is made with a clear beef broth and thin pancake strips that are rolled up and sliced before being added to the soup. The soup is often garnished with chives and is a popular choice for lunch or as a starter before a main course.

Austria also has a long tradition of baking, and there are many sweet treats to choose from. The most famous of these is the Sachertorte, a chocolate cake invented in Vienna in 1832. The cake is made with layers of dense chocolate cake, apricot jam, and chocolate ganache. It's typically served with a dollop of whipped cream and a cup of Viennese coffee.

Another sweet treat that's worth trying is Kaiserschmarrn. This dish is a type of shredded pancake that's typically served with fruit compote or applesauce. The pancake is made with flour, milk, eggs, and sugar and is shredded into small pieces before being caramelized in butter.

Austria is also known for its cheese, and one of the most famous cheeses is Bergkäse. This cheese is made from raw cow's milk and has a nutty and slightly sweet flavor. It's often used in traditional dishes such as Käsespätzle, a type of pasta dish made with cheese, onions, and caramelized onions.

When it comes to drinks, Austria has a long tradition of winemaking. The country's wine regions are scattered throughout the country, and they produce a variety of white and red wines. Some of the most famous wine regions include Wachau, Kamptal, and Burgenland. Grüner Veltliner is one of the most popular white wines from Austria, while Blaufränkisch is a popular red wine.

Austria is also famous for its beer, and there are many local breweries that produce a wide range of beers. One of the most famous beers is Gösser, which has been around since 1860. The brewery offers tours where you can learn about the brewing process and sample some of their beers.

Finally, we have to mention Austria's most famous spirit – Schnaps. This clear fruit brandy is made from various fruits, including apricots, plums, and pears. It's a popular after-dinner drink and is often served in small glasses called "Schnapsgläser."

In addition to these traditional dishes, Austria has also seen a rise in modern and innovative cuisine in recent years. Many restaurants in Austria offer a fusion of traditional and modern dishes, with an emphasis on locally sourced ingredients.

Shopping in Austria

Austria is a country that is well-known for its rich cultural heritage, stunning architecture, and beautiful landscapes. But it's also a great destination for shopping enthusiasts, with plenty of options for all tastes and budgets. From luxury fashion brands to traditional souvenirs, Austria offers a diverse range of shopping experiences that cater to every shopper's preferences.

Vienna, the capital of Austria, is a popular destination for luxury shopping. The city is home to some of the world's most famous high-end fashion brands, including Chanel, Gucci, and Louis Vuitton. The city also has a wide range of department stores, including Steffl, which is located on Kärntner Straße and offers six floors of luxury shopping.

In addition to luxury shopping, Austria is also known for its traditional crafts and souvenirs. These can be found in local markets and shops throughout the country, offering visitors the chance to take home unique and authentic souvenirs. Popular items include handcrafted jewelry, ceramics, and textiles, as well as local food products such as cheese, wine, and chocolate.

Whether you're looking for luxury fashion or traditional souvenirs, Austria offers a shopping experience that is sure to delight.

Souvenirs and gifts

When traveling to Austria, there are a variety of unique and traditional souvenirs and gifts that one can bring back home. From artisanal crafts to food products, there is something for everyone to remember their time in Austria.

One of the most popular souvenirs to bring back from Austria is a traditional dirndl or lederhosen. These traditional garments are worn during festivals and special occasions and can be found in many shops throughout the country. Dirndls are a type of dress that is usually accompanied by an apron, while lederhosen are leather shorts that are often worn with suspenders. Both garments come in a variety of styles and colors, making them a unique and authentic souvenir.

Another popular souvenir is a piece of handcrafted jewelry. Austria is known for its artisans who create unique and intricate pieces using a variety of materials such as Swarovski crystals, pearls, and silver. These pieces can be found in shops throughout the country and make for a special gift to bring back home.

For those with a sweet tooth, Austrian chocolate and sweets make for a delicious souvenir. Austria is famous for its chocolate, with companies such as Zotter and Lindt producing high-quality products. Another sweet treat to bring back is Mozartkugeln, a chocolate-covered marzipan candy that is named after the famous Austrian composer, Wolfgang Amadeus Mozart.

Austrian ceramics are another popular souvenir, with many shops throughout the country offering unique and handcrafted pieces. These ceramics can come in a variety of styles, from traditional designs to more modern and abstract patterns. They can be used as home decor or as functional pieces such as plates or mugs.

Austria is also known for its wine, with many regions throughout the country producing high-quality bottles. For those interested in bringing back a bottle or two, there are many shops that offer wine tasting and can help select the perfect bottle to bring back home. In addition to wine, Austria is also famous for its schnapps, a type of brandy that is made from a variety of fruits.

For those looking for a more practical souvenir, Austrian wool products are a great option. Austria is known for its high-quality wool, with many shops offering items such as scarves, hats, and blankets made from the material. These items are not only practical but also make for a cozy and comfortable reminder of one's time in Austria.

Finally, for those looking for a unique and authentic souvenir, a traditional Austrian musical instrument such as a zither or accordion can be a great option. These instruments have a long history in Austria and are still played today, especially during folk music performances and festivals.

Local markets and fairs

Austria is known for its vibrant local markets and fairs, offering visitors a chance to experience traditional Austrian culture and cuisine. These markets can be found in cities and towns throughout the country, and are a great way to sample local products and purchase unique souvenirs.

One of the most famous markets in Austria is the Naschmarkt in Vienna, which is the largest open-air market in the city. The market offers a variety of fresh fruits and vegetables, meats, cheeses, and other culinary delights, as well as traditional crafts and souvenirs. The market is open daily except for Sundays, and is a popular destination for both tourists and locals alike.

In Salzburg, the traditional farmers' market takes place every Thursday on the Universitätsplatz. The market offers a wide range of fresh produce, as well as local cheeses, meats, and baked goods. It's a great place to sample traditional Austrian cuisine and purchase souvenirs such as handcrafted ceramics and textiles.

Innsbruck also has a vibrant local market scene, with the Innsbruck Christmas Market being one of the most famous. The market takes place in the Old Town during the Advent season, and offers traditional Austrian Christmas decorations, handmade gifts, and hot drinks and food. The market is a popular destination for tourists and locals alike, and is a great way to experience the festive spirit of the city.

Another popular event in Austria is the Graz Spring Fair, which takes place in April each year. The fair offers a variety of traditional crafts, local products, and entertainment, including live music and dance performances. It's a great way to experience the culture of Styria, and to purchase unique souvenirs that can't be found anywhere else.

For those interested in traditional Austrian clothing and textiles, the Kitzbühel Country Fair is a must-visit. The fair takes place every August, and offers a wide range of handcrafted garments, jewelry, and textiles, as well as traditional foods and drinks. The fair is a great place to purchase a unique dirndl or lederhosen, as well as other traditional Austrian clothing and accessories.

In addition to these larger markets and fairs, there are also many smaller markets that take place in towns and villages throughout Austria. These markets offer a more intimate experience, and often specialize in specific products or crafts. For example, the Lienz Farmer's Market in East Tyrol offers a variety of fresh produce and local meats, while the Bad Gastein Craft Market features traditional handcrafted items such as pottery and woodcarvings.

Austria's local markets and fairs offer visitors a chance to experience traditional Austrian culture and cuisine, and to purchase unique and authentic souvenirs. From the Naschmarkt in Vienna to the Graz Spring Fair, there is something for everyone to explore and enjoy. So whether you're a foodie, a fan of traditional crafts, or simply looking for a unique shopping experience, Austria's local markets and fairs are not to be missed.

Luxury shopping

Austria is renowned for its luxury shopping experience, with a variety of high-end boutiques and designer stores scattered throughout the country. Vienna, in particular, is known for its luxury shopping scene, with a range of international and local brands available in the city center.

One of the most prestigious shopping areas in Vienna is the Golden Quarter, which is home to flagship stores for brands such as Louis Vuitton, Prada, and Chanel. The area is known for its opulent architecture and high-end boutiques, and is a popular destination for luxury shoppers from around the world.

Another popular luxury shopping destination in Vienna is the Kärntner Strasse, which is one of the city's main shopping streets. The street is lined with luxury brands such as Gucci, Dior, and Tiffany & Co., as well as traditional Austrian stores selling items such as handmade ceramics and textiles.

In Salzburg, luxury shoppers can visit the Getreidegasse, which is one of the city's oldest and most picturesque shopping streets. The street is lined with high-end boutiques, including the famous

Mozartkugel store, which sells handmade chocolates and souvenirs.

Innsbruck also offers a luxury shopping experience, with a range of high-end boutiques and designer stores located in the city center. The Maria-Theresien-Strasse is a popular destination for luxury shoppers, and is home to brands such as Swarovski and Omega.

For those looking for a more exclusive shopping experience, Austria also offers a variety of luxury department stores. The Steffl department store in Vienna, for example, offers a range of high-end brands and designer collections, as well as a rooftop bar and restaurant with panoramic views of the city.

Austria offers a luxury shopping experience that rivals that of other major European cities. With a variety of high-end boutiques, designer stores, and luxury department stores, visitors can indulge in a range of exclusive shopping experiences while enjoying the country's beautiful architecture and cultural heritage.

UNDERSTANDING

AUSTRIAN CULTURE AND

CUSTOMS

Austria is a country with a rich cultural heritage and a variety of customs and traditions that are celebrated throughout the year. Understanding Austrian culture and customs is important for visitors to the country, as it can enhance their travel experience and help them to better appreciate the local way of life.

One of the most distinctive aspects of Austrian culture is its strong connection to classical music, with composers such as Mozart,

Haydn, and Strauss all hailing from Austria. The country is also known for its traditional folk music, dance, and costumes, which are often performed at festivals and events.

Another important aspect of Austrian culture is its cuisine, which is influenced by the country's location at the crossroads of central Europe. Austrian dishes typically feature meat, potatoes, and dairy products, and are often accompanied by beer or wine.

In addition to music and food, Austrian culture also has a strong tradition of crafts, such as glassblowing, woodcarving, and embroidery. These crafts are often used to create souvenirs and gifts that reflect the country's cultural heritage.

Overall, understanding Austrian culture and customs can help visitors to appreciate the country's unique identity and traditions, and to engage more deeply with the local community.

Annual events and festivals

Austria is known for its rich cultural heritage and hosts many events and festivals throughout the year that celebrate Austrian traditions, customs, and history. These events attract visitors from around the world who come to experience the unique atmosphere and participate in the festivities. Here are some of the most popular annual events and festivals in Austria:

Vienna Opera Ball - February/March

The Vienna Opera Ball is one of the most prestigious events in Austria's cultural calendar. Held annually at the Vienna State Opera, it is a celebration of classical music, dance, and Viennese glamour. The ball attracts thousands of guests from around the world and features a grand opening ceremony, a range of performances, and an opulent dance floor.

Salzburg Festival - July/August

The Salzburg Festival is one of the world's most famous classical music festivals, attracting renowned performers, conductors, and composers from around the world. Held annually in Salzburg, the festival includes performances of opera, drama, and classical music, as well as exhibitions, readings, and discussions.

Innsbruck Christmas Market - November/December

The Innsbruck Christmas Market is a traditional market held in the city's old town during the Advent season. The market features more than 70 stalls selling handmade gifts, Christmas decorations, and traditional Austrian food and drink. There are also daily performances of Christmas carols and other music.

Bregenz Festival - July/August

The Bregenz Festival is an open-air music and arts festival held annually on the shores of Lake Constance. The festival features opera, theater, and concerts, and is known for its spectacular stage designs, which often involve large-scale installations on the lake.

Vienna International Film Festival - October/November

The Vienna International Film Festival is one of the oldest and most respected film festivals in the world. Held annually in Vienna, it features a range of international films, as well as retrospectives, discussions, and exhibitions.

Salzburg Advent Singing - December

The Salzburg Advent Singing is a traditional music event held annually in the city's cathedral. The event features performances by choirs and musicians from around the region, as well as readings and other festive activities.

Vienna Jazz Festival - June/July

The Vienna Jazz Festival is one of Europe's most popular jazz festivals, attracting renowned performers from around the world. The festival features a range of jazz styles, from traditional to contemporary, and takes place at various venues throughout the city.

Tyrolean Festival Erl - July/August

The Tyrolean Festival Erl is an annual music festival held in the small village of Erl, located in the Tyrolean Alps. The festival features a range of classical music performances, as well as readings, exhibitions, and discussions.

Vienna Music Film Festival - July/August

The Vienna Music Film Festival is an open-air festival held annually in Vienna's Rathausplatz. The festival features a range of music films, from classical to rock and pop, and is free to attend.

Villach Carnival - February

The Villach Carnival is a traditional carnival held annually in the city of Villach. The carnival features parades, costumes, and music, and is known for its humorous and satirical floats and performances.

Social Norms And Etiquette

Austria is a country with a strong sense of tradition and etiquette, and visitors to the country should be aware of these social norms in order to avoid causing offense or confusion. Here are some of the key social norms and etiquette in Austria:

1. Greetings and Introductions

Austrians are typically formal when meeting new people, and it is customary to use formal titles such as "Herr" or "Frau" when addressing someone. Handshakes are common when greeting people, and it is important to make eye contact and offer a sincere greeting.

2. Dining Etiquette

Austrian dining etiquette is similar to that of other European countries, with a few key differences. It is polite to wait for the host to offer a toast before beginning to drink, and it is customary to keep your hands visible on the table during the meal. It is also considered impolite to leave food on your plate, so it is better to take smaller portions if you are unsure of how much to eat.

3. Dress Code

Austrians place a high value on appearance and dressing appropriately for different occasions. In general, casual dress is acceptable for everyday activities, but it is important to dress more formally for business meetings, cultural events, and religious services.

4. Punctuality

Austrians place a strong emphasis on punctuality, and it is considered impolite to be late for appointments or meetings. If you are running late, it is important to call or send a message to let the other person know.

5. Personal Space

Austrians tend to have a smaller personal space than people from other cultures, and it is common to stand closer together when speaking. However, it is still important to respect personal boundaries and not to invade someone's personal space without permission.

6. Politeness and Respect

Austrians place a high value on politeness and respect, and it is important to use appropriate language and behavior in all social situations. This includes avoiding loud or aggressive behavior, using "please" and "thank you" when making requests, and showing respect for religious and cultural traditions.

7. Tipping

Tipping is customary in Austria, but it is not expected to be as generous as in some other countries. In general, a tip of 5-10% is considered appropriate for good service, and it is not necessary to leave a tip for bad service.

Overall, understanding social norms and etiquette in Austria can help visitors to navigate social situations with ease and avoid causing offense or confusion. By showing respect for Austrian traditions and customs, visitors can enhance their travel experience and build positive relationships with the local community.

History and Traditions

Austria has a rich history and cultural heritage that dates back thousands of years. The country's location at the crossroads of Europe has played a key role in shaping its history and traditions, and has led to a unique blend of influences from different cultures and civilizations.

The earliest known inhabitants of Austria were the Celts, who arrived in the area in the 5th century BCE. They were followed by the Romans, who established a province in the region in the 1st century BCE. During the Middle Ages, Austria was ruled by various noble families, including the Babenbergs and the Habsburgs, who established a powerful empire that lasted for centuries.

One of the most significant events in Austrian history was the reign of Empress Maria Theresa in the 18th century. She initiated a series of reforms that modernized the country's administration, education, and economy, and laid the foundations for Austria's emergence as a major European power.

Austria is also known for its rich cultural traditions, which are influenced by its long history and diverse cultural heritage. Classical music has played a particularly important role in Austrian culture, with renowned composers such as Mozart, Beethoven, and Schubert all hailing from the country. Austria is also known for its traditional folk music, dance, and costumes, which are often performed at festivals and events.

In addition to music, Austria has a strong tradition of crafts, such as glassblowing, woodcarving, and embroidery. These crafts are often used to create souvenirs and gifts that reflect the country's cultural heritage.

Another important aspect of Austrian culture is its cuisine, which is influenced by the country's location at the crossroads of central Europe. Austrian dishes typically feature meat, potatoes, and dairy products, and are often accompanied by beer or wine. Some of the most famous Austrian dishes include Wiener schnitzel, apple strudel, and Sachertorte.

Austria also has a rich tradition of Christmas markets, which are held in cities and towns throughout the country during the holiday season. These markets feature traditional crafts, food, and drink, and are a popular destination for locals and tourists alike.

Overall, Austria's history and traditions are an important part of the country's identity and culture. Understanding and appreciating these traditions can enhance visitors' travel experience and help them to better appreciate the country's unique cultural heritage.

CONCLUSION

Austria is a country that offers visitors a unique blend of history, culture, and natural beauty. From the stunning Alpine landscapes to the vibrant cities and rich cultural traditions, there is something for everyone in Austria.

For those interested in history and culture, Austria's cities offer a wealth of museums, galleries, and historic sites to explore. Vienna, in particular, is known for its elegant architecture, rich musical heritage, and vibrant cultural scene. Salzburg, the birthplace of Mozart, is another popular destination for culture lovers, with its well-preserved old town and famous music festivals.

For nature enthusiasts, Austria's mountains, lakes, and forests offer endless opportunities for hiking, skiing, and outdoor adventures. The country's national parks and protected areas are home to a diverse range of wildlife and plant species, and offer a chance to connect with nature in a peaceful and serene environment.

Food and drink are also an important part of the Austrian experience, with the country's cuisine reflecting its unique cultural heritage and location at the crossroads of Europe. Traditional dishes like Wiener schnitzel, apple strudel, and Sachertorte are a must-try for foodies, while the country's beer and wine are also highly regarded.

Overall, Austria is a country that offers something for everyone, whether you're interested in history, culture, nature, or simply want to relax and enjoy the scenery. With its friendly people, safe environment, and excellent transportation and infrastructure, it's also an ideal destination for travelers of all ages and interests. The Austria travel experience is sure to be a memorable one that will leave visitors with a deep appreciation for this fascinating country.

Tips For Travelers To Austria

If you're planning a trip to Austria, there are a few tips and tricks that can help you make the most of your experience. From practical advice on transportation and accommodations to cultural tips on etiquette and local customs, these tips for travelers to Austria can help ensure a smooth and enjoyable trip.

I. Plan your transportation in advance

Austria has a well-developed transportation system, with trains, buses, and trams connecting the country's major cities and towns. However, it's important to plan your transportation in advance, as schedules and routes can vary depending on the time of year and other factors. It's also a good idea to book tickets in advance to save money and avoid long lines at ticket counters.

II. Respect local customs and etiquette

Austria has a unique culture and set of customs that visitors should be aware of. For example, it's considered rude to be late for appointments or meetings, and punctuality is highly valued. It's also important to dress appropriately for the occasion, with formal attire often required for events like concerts and operas. Additionally, it's considered impolite to ask personal questions or discuss sensitive topics like politics or religion.

III. Learn some basic German phrases

While many Austrians speak English, it's always a good idea to learn some basic German phrases to help navigate daily interactions. This can include greetings, asking for directions, and ordering food at restaurants. Even a few words of German can go a long way in establishing a friendly rapport with locals.

IV.   Take advantage of local markets and festivals

Austria is known for its vibrant markets and festivals, which offer a chance to experience local culture and cuisine. From the famous Christmas markets in Vienna and Salzburg to the summer music festivals in Salzburg and Bregenz, there's always something happening in Austria. Be sure to check the calendar of events for your visit and plan accordingly.

V.   Don't forget to tip

Tipping is customary in Austria, with a general guideline of 10% for restaurants and cafes. It's also common to round up the bill when paying for services like taxis or haircuts. However, it's important to note that service charges are often included in the bill, so be sure to check before tipping.

VI.   Dress appropriately for the weather

Austria's climate can vary widely depending on the season and location. In the winter, temperatures can drop below freezing and snowfall is common, while summers can be hot and humid. It's important to dress appropriately for the weather, with warm layers in the winter and light, breathable clothing in the summer.

VII.   Bring comfortable shoes

Austria is a country that's best explored on foot, with many attractions and sights within walking distance of each other. It's important to bring comfortable shoes for sightseeing and walking, especially if you plan to explore the country's mountainous regions.

VIII.   Be respectful of the environment

Austria's natural beauty is one of its biggest attractions, and it's important to be respectful of the environment while exploring the country. This can include following designated trails and not littering, as well as being mindful of wildlife and plant species.

IX.   Be aware of safety precautions

Austria is a safe country with low crime rates, but it's still important to be aware of safety precautions while traveling. This can include keeping valuables secure and being vigilant in crowded areas like train stations and markets.

X.   Relax and enjoy the experience

Finally, it's important to relax and enjoy the experience while traveling in Austria. The country's laid-back atmosphere and beautiful scenery can be a refreshing change of pace for visitors, and there's always something new to discover. Whether you're exploring the cities, hiking in the mountains, or sampling local cuisine, take the time to savor the moment.

Printed in Great Britain
by Amazon